ROY FISHER

The Thing About Joe Sullivan
poems 1971-1977

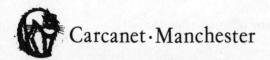
Carcanet · Manchester

Acknowledgements are due to the editors of the following publications, where some of these poems first appeared: *Antaeus, Montemora, Lettera, Stand, Poetry Review, Grosseteste Review, Samphire, Palantir, Meantime*. A number of the poems were broadcast on the BBC 'Poetry Now' programme. Acknowledgement is also due to the Poetry Book Society for poems included in their Supplements, and to PEN *New Poems*.

Some of the work has appeared in pamphlet form: *19 Poems and an Interview* (Grosseteste), *Bluebeard's Castle* (Circle), *Also* (Tetrad), *Barnardine's Reply* (Sceptre), *Epitaphs for Lorine* (Jargon), and *Madeira and Toasts for Basil Bunting's 75th Birthday* (Jargon).

SBN 85635 255 1

First published in 1978 by
Carcanet New Press Limited
330 Corn Exchange
Manchester M4 3BG

The publisher acknowledges the financial assistance of the Arts Council of Great Britain.

Printed in Great Britain by Billings, Guildford

THE THING ABOUT JOE SULLIVAN

JOE SULLIVAN 1906-1971

musician

Roy Fisher

21.v.88

CONTENTS

6

TIMELESSNESS OF DESIRE

Into the purpose: or out.
There is only, without a tune,
timelessness of desire.

don't open up the way
this town shines in through glass
and the days darken;
there's nothing better,
not one thing better to do—

What's now only disproved
was once imagined.

IF I DIDN'T

If I didn't dislike
mentioning works of art

I could say
the poem has always
already started, the parapet
snaking away, its grey line guarding
the football field and the sea

—the parapet
has always already started
snaking away, its grey line
guarding the football field and the sea

and under whatever progression
takes things forward

there's always
the looking down
between the moving frames

into those other movements
made long ago or in some
irrecoverable scale
but in the same alignment
and close to recall.

Some I don't recognize,
but I believe them—

one system of crimson scaffolding,
another, of flanges—

All of them must be mine,
the way I move on:

and there I am,
half my lifetime back,
on Goodrington sands
one winter Saturday,

troubled in mind: troubled
only by Goodrington beach
under the gloom, the look of it
against its hinterland

and to be walking
acres of sandy wrack,
sodden and unstable
from one end to the other.

AT ONCE

I say at once there's a light on the slope among the allot-
ment huts. If I leave it a moment unsaid it'll set solid, and
that only the beginning. But, said, it has gone.

The wonderful light, clear and pale like a redcurrant, is set
off by a comfortable mist of winter afternoon over to one
side of it among the allotment gardens.

Appearance of mist. The light in its glass. The witnesses
were built in about 1910 in the shapes of houses. The
stream crawls past the bottom of the slope, edged with
vegetables and crossed by planks. You can approach.

The light is in the earth if anywhere. This is already the
place where it was. We've hardly started, and I want to do
it again.

DIVERSIONS

1.
Trouble coming, on a Saturday or a Monday,
some day with a name to it:

staining the old paths trouble knows,
though I forget them.

2.
Walk through, minding the nettles
at the corner of the brick path—

don't feel sorry for language, it doesn't bear
        talking about.

3.
Built for quoting in a tight corner—
The power of dead imaginings to return.

4.
Just beside my track through the dark,
my own dark, not to be described,
the screech-owl
sounds, in his proper cry
and in all his veritable image—
you would know him at once.

Beyond him
a dissolution of my darkness
into such forms
as live there in the space
beyond the clear image of an owl:

forms without image;
pointless to describe.

5.

I saw what there was to write and I wrote it.
When it felt what I was doing, it lay down and died under
    me.

6.

Grey weather beating across the upland,
and the weather matters.
Grey weather beating easily across the upland.

7.

Crooked-angle wings
blown sideways
against the edge of the picture.

8.

Roused from a double
depth of sleep, looking up
through a hole in the sleep's surface above;
no sense of what's there;
a luminous dial
weaves along the dark like a torch.
There's somebody already
up and about, a touch-paper crackle
to their whispering.

9.

The kites are the best sort of gods,
mindless, but all style;

even their capriciousness,
however dominant,
not theirs at all.

Lost from its line
one flies steadily out to sea,
its printed imperturbable face
glinting as it dips and rises
dwindling over the waves.

The crowd on the shore
reach out their hearts.

10.

Leaden August with the life gone out of it,
not enough motion
to shift old used-up things.

A bad time to be rid of troubles,
they roll back in.

Dead troubles take longer than live ones.

11.

The pilgrim disposition—
walking in strung-out crowds
on exposed trackways
as if ten yards from home:

domestic to-ing and fro-ing
uncoiled and elongated
in a dream of purpose.

12.

Then some calm and formal portrait
to turn a level gaze
on the milling notions,

its tawniness of skin denoting
tension maybe, a controlled pallor;

or a blush of self-delight
welling softly from its intelligence.

13.
Periodicity: the crack
under the door of this room
as I stare at it, late at night,
has the same relation to its field
as—what?

The corner over the curtain-rail
in a room I was in one night
forty years ago and more.

The light and the height are different,
and so am I;
but something in the staring
comes round again.

So I stare
at the single recurrence of a counter
I expect never to need.

14.
Sliding the tongue-leaved
crassula arborescens
smartly in its pot and saucer
from one end of the windowsill
right down to the other

alters the framed view, much
as a louvred shutter would.

All my life I've been left-handed.

15.
Here comes the modulation.
Elbows in, tighten up:
a sucked-in, menacing sound,
but full. The space is narrow,
the time marked out,
and everybody's watching.

16.
The woman across the lane
stoops, hands on knees,
behind out, black and grey hair
falling forward, her nose level
with the top of a four foot wall
under a huge shaggy bank of privet.

Nose to nose with her across a saucer,
his tail lifting into the privet shadow,
a big dark cat with a man's
face marked out in white.

Quietly,
in a good, firm Scottish voice,
set well down,
she tells his story:
                                    how
when his owners first
moved another cat in on him
then moved out altogether,
he ran wild for three years,
haunting back once in a while,
a frightener.

After that
for a year and a half
she'd set for him daily,
slowly drawing him in

as near as this;
she didn't expect more.

She talks, and the cat drinks.
He turns his mask to me,
sees me, and without pausing
vanishes.

      Later, from a distance,
I see the two of them again,
a saucer apart. The cat
with his enormous guilt
and importance;
           the fortunate cat,
to have such a calm Scots lady
to understand his importance.

  17.
Out to one side
a flight of shops
turning towards the sun,

each one a shallow step higher,
white and new and good.

And there's the ultimate in shops;
the gallery.

Somebody can be stood—
can elect to stand—
in fresh clothes but barefoot
on a slate ledge, in the place of a pot,

fastidious
beyond the flakings of the skin,
the vegetable variants of body-form,

the negative
body-aura,
that shadowy khaki coat.

Can stand, and receive attributions
of pain and excellence.

18.
*Everything cast in iron
must first be made in wood—*

The foundry patternmaker
shapes drains, gears,
furnace doors, couplings
in yellow pine.

His work fulfils the conditions for myth:
it celebrates origin,
it fixes forms for endless recurrence;
it relates energy to form;
is useless in itself;

for all these reasons it also attracts
aesthetic responses in anybody
free to respond aesthetically;

and it can be thought with;

arranged on trays in the Industrial Museum,
it mimes the comportment
of the gods in the Ethnology cases.

19.
Outlines
start to appear
on the milky surface.

Points first,
quickening into perimeters
branches and dividers;
an accelerating wonder.

Arrest; try lifting it away
before the creation
diversifies totally
to a deadlocked fission:
diamond-faceted housebricks
in less than light.

The thin trace lifted off will drop
into a new medium and dissolve.
On the bland surface
will appear new outlines.

Both these ways are in nature.

20.
A world
arranged in zones
outside and into
this waterfront café.

A strip of sky
misty with light,

a deep band of
dark hazy mountainside,

a whole estuary width
foreshortened almost to nothing,

a quay,
a full harbour;

then a pavement,
a sill,

the table where I sit,
and the darkness in my head.

Everything still along its level

except the middle zone, the harbour water,
turbulent with the sunlight
even in calm air.

EPITAPH: LORINE NIEDECKER

Certain trees
came separately from the wood

and with no special
thought of returning

THE LEAST

The least, the meanest,
goes down to less;
there's never an end.

And you can learn
looking for less
and again, less;
your eyes don't get sharper.

For there is less
eyesight;
and no end to that.

There is you,
there is less-you:
the merest trace—
less-eyes will find it.

SOME LOSS

Being drawn again
through the same moment

helpless, and to find
everything simpler yet:

more things I forgot to remember
have gone; maybe because I forgot.

Instead there is blankness
and there is grace:

the insistence of the essential,
the sublime made lyrical
at the loss of what's forgotten.

A POEM NOT A PICTURE

On a ground remarkable for lack of character, sweeps of direction form.

It's not possible to determine whether they rise from the ground's qualities or are marked on to it. Or whether, if the first, the lines suck the ground's force up, or are its delegates; or if the second, whether the imposed marks mobilize or defeat it; or both, in all cases.

Out of a scratch ontology the sweeps of direction form, and, as if having direction, produce, at wide intervals, the events.

These are wiry nodes made of small intersecting planes as if rendered by hatching, and having a vapid, played-out look. But they are the nearest the field has to intense features. Each has a little patch of red.

THE SIGN

First I saw it in colour, then I killed it.
What was still moving, I froze.
That came away. The colour all went
to somebody else's heaven, may they
live on in blessedness. What
came to my hand was fragile, beautiful
and grey, a photograph twilight;
so little to decay there, yet it would
be going down, slowly, be
going down.

THE ONLY IMAGE

Salts work their way
to the outside of a plant pot
and dry white.

        This encrustation
is the only image.
          The rest—
the entire winter, if there's winter—
comes as a variable that shifts
in any part, or vanishes.

           I can
compare what I like to the salts,
to the pot, if there's a pot,
to the winter if there's a winter.

The salts I can compare
to anything there is.
Anything.

SIMPLE LOCATION

In simple location
the sticks take fire:

they cross and tangle
with smoke-spurts

breaking into the sunlight
as it strikes the ground,

coming in from a fog-rim
through the bleached grasses;

and if a golden drop escapes
anywhere on the skin

of a boy I've seen starting to sweat
in my dream

it has its place—
or if it should leave his eye

by way of the honey-crust there
and slowly trickle

down by the corner of his mouth
to undo everything:

if the sense of charged confinement
should come again

it seizes on a breath
caught in its place in the body,

held there a moment; still
filled with the fire-scents.

DARK ON DARK

Dark on dark—
they never merge:

the eye imagines to separate them,
imagines to make them one:

imagines the notion of impossibility
for eyes.

MOUTH TALK

Mouth of artifice
fashioned to make
mouth-talk.

Not formal. Familiar.

The tablecloth
　　　falls,
　　　　　　legs
rest on the floor;
　　　draperies of the design
everywhere of the most temporary:

it is made.

It has motion:
　　　the floor a wind
propelled by the thought of a fan—

　　　　(happy the world so made
　　　　as to be
　　　　blessed by the modes of art)

driven by fan blades
and their dark eddies,
　　　wave-patterns that convert
into mouth-talk.

A GRAMMAR FOR DOCTRINE

Not what
neutralizes by balance
or by extension cancels—

This is the cleft:
rate it how you will,
as an incredible thing
with tangible properties, even.
But without doubt
the thing that is
shown to people.

Real emphasis
only in the plainness of the signs
for what's known;

mystification itself,
eternal sport,
opens a coloured arch,
plastic to the core,

and a tram with little decoration

sends courageous Gaudi to Avernus.
Entry is quick, you never sense it,

return by way of what's known:
entry is quick, you never sense it,
however you repeat it, or hang by a hair.

CORNER

Dark projecting corner
of shiny mahogany
standing out
among shadowy walls.

Beside it the face
gleams. Somebody standing

or halted in walking out.
A teacher—
                there are no
teachers here, no lessons.
It's not a teacher.
                    Somebody—
the settings are made
to show faces off.
People have to expect to be seen.
They can clear themselves of enigma
if the settings allow,
if the enigma—

Keats's death-mask
a face built out from a corner.

If you're living
any decor
can make a wraith of you.

WISH

That, once sighted,
it should move of its own accord,

right out of view most likely;

and if it does that
a more primitive state altogether
gets revealed:
               a hardened
paste-patch
of rhubarb and mud-green.

—here comes morning again,
sunshine out of an egg—

and where the first sight
was all design
               what's left
shows its behind,
stamps and wiggles,
resists transference,
won't be anybody's currency;
doesn't aim to please
and for the most part doesn't.

WITHOUT LOCATION

A life without location—
just the two of us
maybe, or a few—

keeping in closeup:
and the colours—
and just the colours

coming from the common source
one after the other
on a pulse;

and passing around us,
turning about and
flaking to form a world,

patterning on the need for a world
made on a pulse.
That way we keep the colours,

till they break and go
and leave no trace; nothing
that could hold an association.

ON THE OPEN SIDE

On the open side, look out
for sun-patches of sea-blue:

if you see them
it's beginning to shift
with factory towers along the edge,
chalk-white and silver,
empty even of machines

—the other life,
the endless other life,
endless beyond the beginning;

that holds and suddenly presents
a sunny day twenty years ago,
the open window of a train
held up on an embankment for an hour:

down the field there were children playing
round a concrete garage.
That was all. Something the other life wanted—
I hadn't kept it.

But look out
for the sea-blue patches.
They'll not make problems.

THE TRACE

Although at first it was single
and silver

it travelled as ink falls
through cold water

and gleamed in a vein
out of a darkness

that turned suddenly on its back
and was dusty instead

letting go forth as it must
a plummet of red wax

from whose course when they lost it
rings of dull steel

like snake ribs in a sidelong curve
twisted away and lifted

to clamp on to a concrete
precipice broken with rust

and with shrubby growths
clustering under it

their leaves
shading and silvering

in the currents of light
draining among the branches

to where it was sodden
full of silky swallowed hair

that dried and was
flying in a fan

air flickering from its ends
collecting silvers

as it twined itself
into the gauze

then scattered as many
mercurial bolts

all through the chamber
darting everywhere

in under the roof-keel
with its infinite brown decline

its warp
unmistakable as it reached

down into the daylight
with a sidelong wooden nose

biased like the set
of a rudder and pulling in

everything that could raise
a bright wave against it

making colours print
themselves on to planes with the effort

one plate of red enamel
dominant and persisting

even through a grey
sleet that scored its face

running away as water
welling downwards

through a raised irregular
static vein

moving only by rills
within itself.

EMBLEM

for Basil Bunting

Wing
    torn out of stone
like a paper fan

Hung in a sky
        so hard
the stone seems paper

Bare stems of ivy
      silver themselves
into the stones

And hold up the wall
      like an armature
till they force it apart

HANDSWORTH LIBERTIES

1.
Open—
and away

in all directions:
room at last for the sky
and a horizon;

for pale new towers in the north
right on the line.

It all
radiates outwards
in a lightheaded air
without image;

there is a world.
It has been made
out of the tracks of waves
broken against the rim
and coming back awry; at the final
flicker they are old grass and fences.
With special intensity
they gather and break out
through birch-bark knuckles.

2.
Lazily into the curve,
two roads of similar importance
but different ages, join,

doubling the daylight
where the traffic doubles,
the spaces
where the new cut through

cleared the old buildings back
remaining clear
even when built on.

3.
A thin smoke
in the air as dusk approaches;
unpointed brickwork
lightly soiled,
not new, not old;

papery pink roses
in the smoke.

The place is full of people.
It is thin. They are moving.
The windows
hold up the twilight.
It will be dark, but never deep.

4.
Something has to happen here.
There must be change.
It's the place
from which the old world fell away
leaning in its dark hollow.

We can go there
into the seepage,
the cottage garden with hostas
in a chimneypot

or somewhere here
in the crowd of exchanges
we can change.

5.
From here to there—
a trip between two locations
ill-conceived, raw, surreal
outgrowths of common sense, almost
merging one into the other

except for the turn
where here and there
change places, the moment
always a surprise:

on an ordinary day a brief
lightness, charm between realities;

on a good day, a break
life can flood in and fill.

6.
Tranquility a manner;
peace, a quality.

With not even a whiff of peace
tranquilities ride the dusk
rank upon rank,
the light catching their edges.

Take masonry
and vegetation.
Witness composition
repeatedly.

7.
The tall place
the top to it
the arena with a crowd.

They do things by the roadside
they could have done in rooms,
but think this better,

settling amid the traffic
on the central reservation turf,
the heart of everything
between the trees.

And with style: they bring
midnight and its trappings out
into the sun shadows.

8.
At the end of the familiar,
throwing away the end
of the first energy, regardless;
nothing for getting home with—

if there's more
it rises from under the first
step into the strange
and under the next and goes on
lifting up all the way;

nothing has a history. The most
gnarled things are all new,

mercurial tongues
dart in at the mouth,
in at the ears;

they lick at the joints. It is new,
this moon-sweat; or by day
this walking through groundsel
among cracked concrete foundations

with devil-dung
in the corners.

Newest of all
the loading platform
of a wrecked dairy,
departure point
for a further journey
into the strangest yet—

Getting home—getting home somehow,
late, late and small.

9.
Riding out of the built-up
valley without a view
on to the built-up crest
where a nondescript murky evening
comes into its own

while everybody gets home
and in under the roofs.

A place for the boys,
for the cyclists,
the strong.

10.
A mild blight, a sterility,
the comfort of others'
homecoming
by way of the paved strip
down one side of the lane;

the separate streetlamps lead
through to the new houses,
which is a clear way

flanked silently
by a laundry—
brick, laurels, a cokeheap
across from the cemetery gate—
a printing works and a small
cycle factory; hard tennis courts.

The cemetery's a valley
of long grass set with marble,
separate as a sea;

apart from the pavement
asphalt and grit are spread
for floors; there are railings,
tarred. It is all
unfinished and still.

11.
Hit the bottom and spread out
among towering structures
and total dirt.

The din compelling
but irrelevant
has the effect of a silence

that drowns out spirit noise
from the sunlit cumulus ranges
over the roofs.

On the way to anywhere
stop off at the old furnace—
maybe for good.

12.
Travesties of the world
come out of the fog
and rest at the boundary.

They never come in:
strange vehicles,
forms of outlandish factories
carried by sound through the air,
they stop at the border,
which is no sort of place;
then they go back.

Why do they manifest themselves?
What good does watching for them do?
They come
out of a lesser world.

I shall go with them sometimes
till the journey dissolves under me.

13.
Shines coldly away
down into distance
and fades
on the next rise to the mist.

If you live on a slope, the first
fact is that all
falls before anything rises,
and that can be too far away
for what it's worth. I

never went there.

Somebody else did, and
I went with them;

I didn't know why. I remember
coming a long way back
out of the hollow

where there was nothing to see
but immediacy, a long wall.

14.
A falling away
          and a rejoicing
    soon after the arrivals—
    small, bright, suspicious—
were complete:
          strangers
sizing one another up
in front of the shade.

With the falling away
          the tale finishes.

Before, nobody knew them,
after, there was nothing to know.
They were swept down into the sky
or let to drift along edges
that reached out, finite,
balking the advance, delaying
their disappearance out
into the clear.

15.
No dark in the body
deep as this
        even though the sun
hardens the upper world.
          A ladder
climbs down under the side

in the shadow of the tank
and crosses tarry pools.
                              There are
metals that burn the air;
a deathly blue stain
in the cinder ballast,
and out there past the shade
sunlit rust hangs on the still water.

Deep as we go
into the stink
this is not the base,
not the ground. This
is the entertainment.

   16.
This is where the game gets dirty.
It plays
the illusion
of insecurity.

Shops
give way to hoardings,
the ground rumbles,
the street turns to a bridge—
flare and glitter of a roadway
all wheels and feet.

There's no substance;
but inside all this
there's a summer afternoon
shining in a tired room
with a cast-iron radiator,
pipes for a gas fire:
no carpet. No motion.
No security.

INSCRIPTIONS FOR BLUEBEARD'S CASTLE

for Ronald King

THE PORTCULLIS

Beyond me the common daylight
divides

THE CASTLE

The furthest journey is the journey that stays still
and the light of the sky has come from the world
to be packed for a journey

THE INSTRUMENTS OF TORTURE

Man conceived us, men made us. We work
almost with perfection and we feel no pain.

THE ARMOURY

Provide. That their mouths may bleed into the cinders.
With bronze and steel, provide. With beauty, provide.

THE TREASURE HOUSE

What
the sun touches
shines on forever dead
the dead images of the sun
wonderful

48

THE GARDEN

Whose is the body you
remember in yourself?

THE LAND

The light. The rain. The eye. The rainbow—
horizons form, random and inevitable as rainbows
over bright fields of change

THE LAKE OF TEARS

Day has turned to a silver mirror
whose dead extent the weeping
eyes could never see

THE LAST DOOR

Moonlight the dead image of the day—
here by the light of that last coin
we are alive within an eye:
when the eye closes on us all
it is complete

RULES AND RANGES FOR IAN TYSON

Horizons release skies.

A huge wall has a man's shoulder. In the only representation we have it is mottled with a rash and distorted overall, seen through gelatine.

The Thames with its waterfronts; a fabric with a Japanese Anemone design. They intersect at Chaos.

The force of darkness is hard, rigid, incapable of motion either within its own form or by way of evasion. All the same, it is very difficult to find.

The experience of a wind, as if it were a photogravure made of dots. To be vastly magnified.

To walk along two adjacent sides of a building at once, as of right.

After a fair number of years the distasteful aspects of the whole business become inescapable. Our frustrations will die with us, their particular qualities unsuspected. Or we can make the concrete we're staring at start talking back.

Watch the intelligence as it swallows appearances. Half the left side, a set of tones, a dimension or two. Never the whole thing at once. But we shouldn't need to comfort ourselves with thoughts like this.

Under the new system some bricks will still be made without radio receivers or photo-electric elements. No potential for colour-change, light-emission, variation of density—just pure solid bricks. They'll be special.

A terror ruffling the grass far off, and passing without coming near. Between that place and this the grass is a continuous stretch with no intervening features.

Under the new football rules the goals will be set, not facing each other down a rectangle but at the centres of adjoining sides of a square pitch, and the teams will be arranged for attack and defence accordingly. Some minor changes in rules are bound to be necessary, but there will also be rich variations in styles of play.

Darkness fell, surrounding and separating the hollow breves. They howled and shone all night.

ALSO

for Derrick Greaves

also there was another story/ a bird suddenly crossing a
frame of sky to alter/ I had no window, the darkness
moulded me/ it said the messages were settled/ we must
be crossing a frame of sleep, the sunlit screen over the
matted shadow where the cloud had fallen and gone down
lost among the folds/ and searching for loss more faint
than the first loss/ and then to alter everything by passing
it by, asking nothing, expecting nothing to alter/ alter/
/ also there

BUTTERTON FORD

—But the street is the river—

Not much of a river, and
not much of a street.
Not much call for either
down this end.

They may as well double up,
let the stream slant out of the hill
over the cobbles in a thin race;

a footway for flood-time,
with a little bridge with overflow holes
cut in the coping. Keep the pressure off.

FROM THE 'TOWN GUIDE'

Out in the air, the statue
gets cold. It needs a coat.

The coat must have a face on top
to squint for dandruff on the shoulder.

It always did have trousers,
Remember? And a wife.

—She was a raver, great big
wardroby body. Insatiable. Still is.

She drives a car like that one
by the Conveniences. His epitaph

Stands all about. But on his plinth
read simply: 'The Unknown Alderman'.

OF THE EMPIRICAL SELF AND FOR ME

for M. E.

In my poems there's seldom
any *I* or *you*—

>   you know me, Mary;
>   you wouldn't expect it of me—

The night here is humid:
there are two of us sitting out
on the bench under the window;

>   two invisible ghosts
>   lift glasses of white milk
>   and drink
>   and the lamplight
stiffens the white fence opposite.

A tall man passes
with what looks like a black dog.
He stares at the milk, and says
>   *It's nice to be able*
>   *to drink a cup of*
>   *coffee outside at night . . .*

and vanishes. So—
What kind of a world? Even
love's not often a poem. The night
has to move quickly. Sudden rain.
Thunder bursts across the mountain;
the village goes dark with blown fuses,
and lightning-strokes repeatedly
bang out their own reality-prints
of the same white houses
staring an instant out of the dark.

COMMUTER

Shallow, dangerous, but without sensation:
sun beats in the rear view mirror
with cars squatting in the glare
and coming on. This continues.
Gasholders flicker along the horizon.

Out in all weathers on the test rig
that simulates distance by substituting
a noise drawn between two points;
shallow, my face printed on the windscreen,
profile on the side glass; shallow—

Either I have no secrets
or the whole thing's a secret
I've forgotten to tell myself:
something to make time for on the night run south,
when the dazzle turns to clear black
and I can stare out over the wheel
straight at Orion, printed on the windscreen.

ARTISTS, PROVIDERS, PLACES TO GO

The little figures in the architect's drawing
the sleep of reason begets
little figures.

Nose the car up through the ramps
into a bay, and leave it,
keys in the dash by regulation—
cost-effective:
come back and find it gone,
you got free parking.

The concrete multi-tiers
on the high-rise estate
hold everybody's wagon.
Only they don't. What's left there
their kids tear apart, Monkeyville—
anybody in their right mind would have known it.

Next, the Adventure Playground.

Next, celibate adult males
shipped in from the Homelands for work
sleep on long shelves of concrete,
Unity of Habitation. No damp.

—for that drawing, reduce
Sleepers in the Underground to cosiness,
consider the blanket concession.

And there'll always be a taker
for a forgotten corner out of Breughel
suitable for a bare-buttocked, incontinent,
sunken-cheeked ending. Little figure
settled in there.

IN THE BLACK COUNTRY

Dudley from the Castle keep
looks like a town by Kokoschka,

one town excited
by plural perspectives

into four or five
landscapes of opportunity

each one on offer
under a selection of skies,

and it wheels, dips,
shoulders up, opens away

with clarity and confusion—
Art's marvellous.

THE DIRTY DOZEN

Dirty Nature,
Dirty sea;

Dirty daytime,
Dirty cry;

Dirty melody,
Dirty heart;

Dirty God,
Dirty surprise;

Dirty drumlin,
Dirty design;

Dirty radiance,
Dirty ghost.

THE POET'S MESSAGE

What sort of message—
what sort of man
comes in a message?

I would
get into a message if I could
and come complete
to where I can see
what's across the park:
and leave my own position
empty for you in its frame.

IT IS WRITING

Because it could do it well
the poem wants to glorify suffering.
I mistrust it.

I mistrust the poem in its hour of success,
a thing capable of being
tempted by ethics into the wonderful.

CUT WORM

You're the invention
I invented once before—
I had forgotten.

          I need to invent you now
more than you need to be remembered.

SETS

If you take a poem
you must take another
and another
till you have a poet.

And if you take a poet
you'll take another, and so on,
till finally you get
a civilization: or just
the dirtiest brawl you ever saw—
the choice isn't yours.

3RD NOVEMBER 1976

Maybe twenty of us in the late afternoon
are still in discussion. We're talking
about the Arts Council of Great Britain
and its beliefs about itself. We're baffled.

We're in a hired pale clubroom
high over the County Cricket Ground
and we're a set of darkening heads,
turning and talking and hanging down;

beyond the plate glass, in another system, silent,
the green pitch rears up, all colour,
and differently processed. Across it in olive overalls
three performance artists persistently move
with rakes and rods. The cold sky steepens.
Twilight catches the flats rising out of the trees.

One of our number is abducted
into the picture. A sculptor innocent of bureaucracy
raises his fine head to speak out;
and the window and its world frame him.
He is made clear.

STYLE

for Michael Hamburger

Style? I couldn't begin.
That marriage (like a supple glove
that won't suffer me to breathe)
to the language of one's time
and class. The languages
of my times and classes.
Those intricacies
of self and sign. The power to mimic
and be myself. I couldn't.

I'd rather reach the air
as a version by my friend Michael.
He knows good Englishes.
And he knows the language
language gets my poems out of.

PARAPHRASES

for Peter Ryan

Dear Mr Fisher I am writing
a thesis on your work.
But am unable to obtain
texts. I have articles by Davie, D.,
and Mottram, E.,
But not your Books since booksellers
I have approached refuse to
take my order saying they
can no longer afford to
handle 'this type of business'. It is
too late! for me to change
my subject to the work of a more
popular writer, so please Mr Fisher
you must help me since I face the alternatives
of failing my degree or repaying
the whole of my scholarship money . . .

Dear Mr Fisher although I have been unable
to read much of your work (to get it that is)
I am a great admirer of it and your landscapes
have become so real to me I am convinced I have, in fact,
become you. I have never, however,
seen any photograph of you, and am most curious
to have an idea of your appearance,
beyond what my mirror, of course, tells me.
The cover of your *Collected Poems*
(reproduced in the *Guardian*, November 1971)
shows upwards of fifty faces; but which is yours? Are you
the little boy at the front, and if so have you
changed much since then?

Dear Mr Fisher recently while studying
selections from a modern anthology with
one of my GCE groups I came across your interestingly titled
'Starting to Make a Tree'. After the discussion I felt strongly
you were definitely *holding something back* in this poem
though I can't quite reach it. Are you often in Rugby?
If you are, perhaps we could meet and I could
try at least to explain. Cordially, Avis Tree. PS. Should we
arrange a rendezvous I'm afraid I wouldn't
know who to look out for as I've never unfortunately
seen your photograph. But I notice you were born in 1930
the same year as Ted Hughes. Would I be right
in expecting you to resemble *him*, more or less?

                            —Dear Ms Tree,
It's true I'm in Rugby quite often, but the train
goes through without stopping. Could you fancy standing
outside the UP Refreshment Room a few times so that
I could learn to recognize *you*? If you could
just get hold of my four books, and wave them,
then I'd know it was you. As for my own appearance
I suppose it inclines more to the
Philip Larkin side of Ted Hughes's looks . . .
See if you think so as I go by . . .

Dear Mr Fisher I have been commissioned
to write a short
critical book on your work
but find that although I have a full
dossier of reviews etcetera
I don't have access to your books. Libraries
over here seem just not to have bought them in.
Since the books are quite a few years old now
I imagine they'll all have been remaindered
some while back? Or worse, pulped? So can
you advise me on locating second-hand copies,

not too expensively I hope? Anyway,
yours, with apologies and respect . . .

Dear Mr Fisher I am now
so certain I am you that it is obvious to me
that the collection of poems I am currently working on
       must be
your own next book! Can you let me know—
who is to publish it and exactly when
it will be appearing? I shouldn't like there to
be any trouble over contracts, 'plagiarism'
etcetera; besides which it would be a pity
to think one of us was wasting time and effort.
How far have *you* got? Please help me. I
do think this is urgent . . .

OCCASIONAL POEM 7.1.72

The poets are dying because they are told to die.
What kind of dirt is that? Whose hand
jiggles the nerve, what programme demands it,
what death-train are we on? Not poetry:
some of us drink,
some take the wrong kind of walk
or get picked up in canteens
by killer lays—it's all
tasteless to talk about.
Taste is what death has for the talented. Then
the civilization is filth, its taste
the scum on filth. Then the poets
are going to be moving on out past talent,
out past taste. If taste
gets its gift wrappers on death—well—
out past that, too. There are courts
where nobody ought to testify.

IN THE WALL

The trails of light all start
from unstable origins
that drift in the dark
in every direction

They coil and wave
into the frame

which is the dark

They make loops of lemon,
of brilliant angelica, streams
of shimmering ruby water

And they stop dead. Arrested,
it turns to a wet street.

Drive at the barrier again. It makes
a night, wet with brilliances.

Brilliant with the power of arrest.

—Or stale, muffled, the senses
having no edge:
feeling for the underside,
wakeful. The name
is Charlatan. A trodden place,
a city: the feet have been

everywhere—on the pillows,
across the benches, on to the walls.

Deep under the viaduct arches
the bare earth is barren;
no rain or daylight. It is dead
dirt. The naked foot,

the soft parts
have been set down here too.

              Central
to the world, a toilet cubicle
under the street:
                    a judas-hole
in the door, spikes round the top,
a white crisis-chamber.

        In eight or nine distinct
dried brown spattered arcs
somebody's blood has jetted
the whole height of the tiles.
                              He's quite
gone away now.

In the walls

town gods and household gods
used to stare
                    out of ringed eyes
seeing
what was never to be said

lacking, in any case,
discourse.

A scent with no face
in darkness:

sallow beyond the skin
and through to a lily-of-the-valley odour
sallow satin

lifted in the voice

not looking but breathing fast

shifting little and quick
more sensible than sense allows;

a raid into the unalterable.

Household god
on a hall table,
stage-lit from a streetlamp
through frosted glass:

eyeless, topless clay head,
true human image
thrown up in Leisure Arts,
holds evenly within his form
a loose mess of papers

Can't speak.
Can't read.

STAFFORDSHIRE RED

for Geoffrey Hill

There are still clefts cut in the earth
to receive us living:

the turn in the road, sheer through
the sandstone at Offley
caught me unawares,
and drew me, car and all,
down in the rock

closed overhead with trees
that arched from the walls,
their watery green
lighting ferns and moss-shags.

I had not been looking for the passage,
only for the way;

but being suddenly in
was drawn through slowly

—altering by an age,
altering again—

and then the road dropped me
out into a small, well-wooded
valley in vacancy.
Behind me
was a nondescript cleft in the trees.
It was still the same sunless afternoon,
no north or south anywhere in the sky.
By side roads
I made my way out and round again
across the mildnesses of Staffordshire

where the world changes with every mile
and never says so.

When I came face to face with the entry
I passed myself through it a second time,
to see how it was.

It was as it had been.

The savage cut in the red ridge,
the turn in the traveller's bowels,
by design ancient or not;
the brush-flick of energy
between earth and belly;
the evenness of it. How hard
is understanding? Some things
are lying in wait in the world,
walking about in the world,
happening when touched, as they must.

BARNARDINE'S REPLY

Barnardine, given his life back,
is silent.

       With such conditions
what can he say?

         The talk
is all about mad arrangements, the owners
counting on their fingers,
calling it discourse, cheating,
so long as the light increases,
the prisms divide and subdivide,
the caverns crystallize out into day.

Barnardine,
whose sole insight into time
is that the right day for being hanged on
doesn't exist,
            is given
the future to understand.

It comes
as a free sample from the patentholders;
it keeps him quiet for a while.

It's not the reprieve in itself
that baffles him:
he smelt that coming
well before justice devised it—
                lords
who accept the warrant,
put on a clean shirt,
walk to the scaffold,
shake hands all round,
forgive the headsman,

kneel down and say, distinctly, 'Now!' attract
pickpockets of the mind—

But he's led away
not into the black vomit pit
he came out of
but into a dawn world
of images without words
where armed men, shadows in pewter,
ride out of the air and vanish,
and never once stop to say what they mean:

—thumb with a broken nail
starts at the ear lobe,
traces the artery down,
crosses the clavicle, circles
the veined breast with its risen nipple,
goes down under the slope of the belly,
stretching the skin after it—

    butchered just for his stink,
    and for the look in his eye—

In the grey light of a deserted barn
the Venus, bending to grip the stone sill,
puts up no case for what she's after,
not even a sigh,
but flexes her back.
                No choice for the Adonis
but to mount her wordlessly, like a hunting dog—
    just for her scent
    and for the look in her eye.

Somebody draws
a Justice
on the jail wall;

gagged with its blindfold
and wild about the eyes.

107 POEMS

A scraping in the cokehouse. One red car.
Imperfect science weakens assurances
but swallowing hard brings confidence: fall soft
through to a sunlit verge. Another vision:
stretched out like one expecting autopsy
or showers of sparks across a polished hall.

Swallow all down, to mudstains on the glass;
surmounted by the working, come upon
a sweet for Auntie; for the withdrawn and hurt
something comes sloping upwards, tilts the guard,
then goes across another way: surprise
relaxes from a sideboard in a bottle,
rocks to and fro a while, scores up another—
bottle between the lips—is comforted
into a pointless trip and passes out
finally between two stations, wrapped in yellow.

Sepia slippers in a sepia print,
venerable truth again: it comes direct
and broadens as it comes, is beautiful
if truth is what you want; lies in the blood
and lives on without taint. Magnificent
gorges at sunset! They knew how to live.
They draw us in their footsteps, double-tongued.

To drive under the fog again, and to it,
park by red lights along the road gang's ditch;
changes of *Satin Doll* are getting smothered,
two trumpets and a rhythm section working
carelessly through a roof under the ground;
at twenty past the hour they hit the dirt,
go on across the talk, hit it some more;
a silver surface rears up, wonderful;
somebody scared runs in and turns it over.

Squatting resigned among the rest of it
there's cut and come again; eat anything.
Demolished streets make foregrounds to good skies;
warm hands at rubbish fires, or on a keyboard.
But brightness picks out streaks of signal red,
it's morning. Rumpled, nobody can cope.
What leaks through rotted pipes into the gutter
leaves a long stain that tired arms cannot move,
dispirited by sickness and privation
when peaceful hours have coal dumped under them,
a last delivery, ferried in through sleet.

What's newly made gets treated tenderly;
damage is easy while the aconite
first shows under the window's overhang
and looks well. In the cold light is a refuge,
lying back after breakfast to see birds
flash down the pale grey strip beyond the roof;
and it's a lime-green tent where everything
is fugitive and found, and luminous,
with shadows of a dark track off the calendar
into a depth of sky. Hanging there free,
spiralling down, the ink-trails in the water
that reach the floor and spread. To be well-treated—
a café with net curtains where they bring
coffee or coca-cola to the bedridden—
something to recall on a beleaguered common.
Roads open in succession, windows break;
if both your legs get tired, find a good stick;
slow before lunch, but in the afternoons
Olympic stars perform for invalids
and dark brings in harsh winds and roadside breakdowns;
better to hear of rain on other roofs
or technicolour wrongs worked by hard men.

No choice left but to run, and into it
and back again each time, that being where
the way goes anyhow—so, running

brings it round so much faster, the same dream—
daffodil plastic, various laminates,
children released in yards then sucked away
into an unseen hall; enormous tolerance
somewhere about, and for immediate sky,
hand-lotion-coloured plastic overhead,
the first thing in the world; and back again.
Walking across to the cars in the night air,
everyone slows and vanishes. There'll be
familiar movement when the season dives.
Watch ampelopsis redden the tarred wall;
go straight, and not so fast. The inner sky
is coloured plastic—none the worse for it.

Somewhere the copper pipes a pale gasfitter
left unsecured under the floor tread loose.
The new face might look younger were it not
too harried and too sleepy: there's no time.
Old people go so childish you get scared
thinking about it: someone's moving out.
Under the trees, headlands of alyssum
break through a spring where danger without risk
develops to a style and loses body,
loses its ear for trouble. Ride again.
Desolate sunlit foreshores, visited
and photographed, lie doubly far away;
one more red car gets dealt into the pack;
one guest is laid to rest in his own nature,
his to resist if it should overcome him
travelling in the tracks of a clay lorry
or when the powercut lets the dark back in.

Exhausted, by a different route, twice blessed—
they seem like wooden roses, without yield—
draining the glass again, whatever remains,
past all surprise, repeatedly and strong
though without strength, except to head on out,

surrounded by a street, braced up to feel,
ready for thunder, inescapable change,
the healing of the injured; some idea
of what tradition numbers like these are benched in.

PASSING NEWBRIDGE ON WYE

All the space under the bridge
fills with the light
of the bare ash-trees and the stone:

what glitter the softness has
comes from the February sun
striking across the pebbles of the riverbed;
there's nothing else.

   The pale light bursts
the distance of the valley as if
in a water-drop on a windscreen,
but in a fullness
with no sharp instant of design:
it's not for catching.

                  The turn
towards the south at the bridgehead
dissolves to a state of the air,

a state the road rests into
as it passes over.

So you can be clouded
with clarities in the act
of crossing the undemanding water.

DISCOVERING THE FORM

Discovering the form of vibrancy
in one of the minor hilltops,

the whorl of an ear
twisting somewhere under the turf,
a curve you have to guess at.

In a house out of sight round the shoulder,
out of ordinary earshot,
a desperate mother, shut in with her child,
raves back at it when it cries,
on and on and on, in misery and fear.

Round on the quiet side of the hill
their shrieks fill an empty meadow.

THE THING ABOUT JOE SULLIVAN

The pianist Joe Sullivan,
jamming sound against idea

hard as it can go
florid and dangerous

slams at the beat, or hovers,
drumming, along its spikes;

in his time almost the only
one of them to ignore

the chance of easing down,
walking it leisurely,

he'll strut, with gambling shapes,
underpinning by James P.,

amble, and stride over
gulfs of his own leaving, perilously

toppling octaves down to where
the chords grow fat again

and ride hard-edged, most lucidly
voiced, and in good inversions even when

the piano seems at risk of being
hammered the next second into scrap.

For all that, he won't swing
like all the others;

disregards mere continuity,
the snakecharming business,

the 'masturbator's rhythm'
under the long variations:

Sullivan can gut a sequence
in one chorus—

—approach, development, climax, discard—
and sound magnanimous.

The mannerism of intensity
often with him seems true,

too much to be said, the mood
pressing in right at the start, then

running among stock forms
that could play themselves

and moving there with such
quickness of intellect

that shapes flaw and fuse,
altering without much sign,

concentration
so wrapped up in thoroughness

it can sound bluff, bustling,
just big-handed stuff—

belied by what drives him in
to make rigid, display,

shout and abscond, rather
than just let it come, let it go—

And that thing is his mood:
a feeling violent and ordinary

that runs in among standard forms so
wrapped up in clarity

that fingers following his
through figures that sound obvious

find corners everywhere,
marks of invention, wakefulness;

the rapid and perverse
tracks that ordinary feelings

make when they get driven
hard enough against time.

DUSK

The sun sets
in a wall that holds the sky.

You'll not
be here long, maybe.

The window
filled with reflections
turns on its pivot;

beyond its edge
the air goes on cold and deep;
your hand feels it,
or mine, or both;
it's the same air for ever.

Now reach across the dark.

Now touch the mountain.